Copyright ©2022 By Dada Aum Ra. All rights reserved under the Pan American and International Copyright Conventions. This book may not be reproduced, in whole or in part in any form or by any means electronic or mechanical. including photocopying, recording, or by any information storage and retrieval system now known or here after invented without permission from publisher Inner Peace Awareness LLC.

Cover design, illustration, and words by Dada Aum Ra
ISBN # 979-8-9870278-2-0

Dedication

Elizabeth
Louis
Alvin
Steve

John

"To be more childlike, you don't have to give up being an adult. The fully integrated person is capable of being both an adult and a child simultaneously. Recapture the childlike feelings of wide-eyed excitement, spontaneous appreciation, cutting loose, and being full of awe and wonder at this magnificent universe."

Wayne Dyer

Acknowledgments

As with any venture that thrives best based on honest feedback from others, Glorious Meditates is part of that club. Our eyes can be temperamental, seeing as they choose when they want to. Words spelled incorrectly may be caught on the first few reads. I find that after a couple of reads of my own work, no matter how I try, I am not reading it any more because, (in my mind)), I know what I wrote. This becomes an experience of missing obvious mistakes. For me, there are only two solutions for this. If it is only me, I have to wait until I forget what I wrote to ensure I read freshly with curiosity. Secondly, and obviously the best option is to ask for help. One of my dearest friends, Dr. Corigan Malloy, thankfully helped me the most with reading my work. Initially she was the editor of my manuscript. However, as creatives do, I changed this book so much, that the minimum of what she edited is there. Knowing that I take artistic liberties with words and concepts, in case I made a cringe-no she didn't-mistake, I proceeded on my own. I knew it would become annoying and too cumbersome to constantly communicate back and forth with me making changes here and there, sometimes everyday. I was waiting for the "click" that serves as my internal acknowledgement to proceed to the next step.

Cori's style of politely guiding me by saying something to the effect of "people often write ... Not realizing ... is the way to write it" is always appreciated. My stubbornly creative self decided if there is any of "that" in Glorious Meditates" it will stay. So, I thank Cori for all her support. I thank Beatrice Bradford, and her grandson Amooris who read the sample on my iPad while in the car. I believe he was in third grade at the time. His sincere interest was so valuable, his response assisted me with defining Glorious' audience. Marissa Sky, his younger sister, had slight interest, her response was also helpful. As well were the random customers of varying ages, who I showed pages to in Barnes & Noble stores in Florida. Thank you Nathalie Faulk and Jayeesha Dutta for patiently reading through every page along with me in its raw form one day while we were hanging out. The, "this isn't quite clear to me" type of responses were much appreciated. I thank Amy, (co-owner with her husband Dave) of Herbs & Earth in Northwood Florida, who read my proof while running her establishment and found errors that I, (in my "too close to really read it" mode), didn't catch. Others gave me emotional support, Marita Palmer, Dwana Makeba, Julie Rainbow, and Barbara Learner. Please accept my apologies if I forgot anyone. It has been a very long road, with technical and communication setbacks that made me step away for a while and regroup, often. Lastly, I am so grateful for the Adobe InDesign Support team. Gratitude and appreciative thanks to all, including the rest of existence. Peace.

Forward

Glorious Meditates is written and formatted to provide a path for awakening, building, and strengthening your feel-good emotions. This book is to serve as a doorway for giving yourself permission to dream and to travel on a visual journey that exists to uplift you. There is a bombardment of information available at your fingertips every day that provides the exact opposite experience. And, like children on a playground with bullies who tend to attack those enjoying life, there is a message that being uplifted is not fun. That it is not the norm. That you are expected to be unhappy, violent, sad, and jealous of others. We know innately that that is not the case. It is easier to be happy, it takes less work to feel good, because at our core, good vibes thrive. Other emotions are brain feelings. We are so used to working on things mentally that it feels like the normal thing to do. It is a process that enforces the belief that we are guided by our brains. Feed by an onslaught of negativity as a norm, it is not surprising that many of us feel if something comes too easily there is something wrong. Accepting this thought process, we can think like that often. These thoughts mentally cause confirming experiences to come alive in our lives either to us or before our eyes..

Take a breath, take another one. Unless you have breathing issues, or environmental problems surrounding you. You can take as many breaths as you want without a second thought. Easy, right? How about blinking or moving your eyes; more things done without thinking. We do so much automatically, so often, that we usually do not feel ourselves going through the motions, even as they occur. Easy, to see the easy, right? One more, what are your hands doing right now? Are you telling them to do that? Could you imagine what your world would be like if your hands moved only when you consciously told them to? It could be something as simple as thinking "touch my phone screen". You do these actions so often, so smoothly, with ease, that they aren't usually consciously acknowledged. We have more ease of life than we do strife. It is so easy that we often embrace them as isms, optimism, altruism, humanism etc., perspectives that are not treated as being needed or invited to be in discussions.

How one sees is how they experience everything. Like the story of the blind men who are each touching a different part of an elephant, what one sees is their truth. What one experiences is their truth. Another's truth follows the same guidelines. This is, across the board, a given, unless an untruth is intentionally told as a truth. Even in those cases, all parties involved decide how their role in the situation will be portrayed. One can align with their core or, if their brain has another suggestion, one can ignore their core knowingly; on whatever level their knowingness sits. Why, one can also lie invitingly inspiring others to join in, initiating a lie that grows and becomes accepted as a truth that trends and runs side by side true trends.

Trends come and go. Humanity is here to progress regardless of what the popular conversation is at the time. Some things/people are timeless. Micheal Jackson & Prince fall into that category for many, they are examples of lacking limitation in the critical thinking area.. We tend to have limiting expectations of our purpose when aligning with where we mentally and physically live. To some, it is unsettling to conceive of our connection with the Earth and the Universe, even though that is where we live. There was a time when we thought we could drop off the edge of the Earth. Are we relatively much further along in mindset now? We live on a planet that rotates in space to sustain us. It constantly rotates in one direction to provide us with sustainable living. Even those who consider us living a different type of experience, have to agree there is a sustainable set up in place for us to have a healthy existence.

Yet, societally, we, do not embrace the implications of our existence from that perspective. This is not about traveling into space, or documenting what's in Earth's center, or using instruments to decode the Universe. Our opportunity is to take time to feel self. To feel the I Am of who we are to the point of being comfortable with being. To also feel what our bodies do and don't want, and to recognize what inspires us. To grab hold of that recognition and to feel it from our hearts. (Yes, from our hearts. The HeartMath institute has scientifically proven that our heart has more power over our lives than our brains.

Imagine following the trend of that implication.)

What then? After that, eventually, our awareness opens to the point of feeling external influences because of increased sensitivity. What does that look like? Well, this is not a defined science in the cookie cutter sense. Just as every single person on this planet is distinct, even twins, so are our awareness capabilities. Everyone gets to increase their level of sensitivity from their own beginning point, at their own pace. It is not a competition, and comparison is to serve as a gauge of where one is on their journey; a means to collaborate or to recognize a gift of another. This is a beautiful process. All begin similarly with recognition that there is an expanded experience of life available. Embracing that concept without bias is a key. It allows you to get to the next step of recognizing and embracing the fact that others, too, have the option to increase their sensitivity. This is where appreciation of meditation comes in. Meditation quiets the mind. When the mind is quiet, a form of distraction is diminished, consciously observable..

One of our biggest opportunities to take when getting started, is to see the world from a larger perspective. This is similar to being at an event where there are many large booths to step into with exclusive experiences.

Some booths promise adventurous experiences of a lifetime. Some offer love expertise. Others promise the ability to be rich, and so on. You enter some and you can tell if they affect you or not immediately. The ones that don't are quickly forgotten. The ones that do may stay in your mind, possibly to the point of influencing decisions you make in life.

These influences may be recognized at first. However, after a while, when time has passed, you might not notice the influences as much. Once not noticed, influences come across as your own thoughts, shrinking your perspective to their theme.

Now, imagine the booths as life experiences, such as hobbies, people you interact with, and places you go. Some of those experiences are enjoyable, others not so much. The difference between life and the event is that life experiences, good and bad, tend to stay in your thoughts, influencing you. The ability to quiet the mind allows you the ability to recognize the difference between your thoughts and influenced thoughts. It is not a eureka moment. It is like a muscle you build. It stays strong and develops with use. Lack of use provides the option to rebuild its strength any time you prefer.

Way Back

There was a time when families would sit together and enjoy a book. Perhaps it would be a lazy afternoon. Maybe a stormy day, and it's decided to take some downtime from screens as a family and enjoy an activity together. It could be that you want to have family time because it feels like the thing to do. The holidays can bring expectations of these types of connections. Quality time is healthy for the body, and mind. It is good to step away from everyday experiences for moments of relaxation, laughter, introspection, conversation, listening; you get the gist. The future may unfold to reveal what a great idea that was because one member is no longer around for whatever reason. That's when retrospective appreciation of trusting your gut may kick in. It could be as simple as a family member moving shortly after the gathering and not having the opportunity to visit before leaving. Someone's health may cloud situations where effective communication is questionable. Factors can come from anywhere. Life can be unpredictable. This is the step when observing the world from a larger perspective becomes an exciting opportunity. Getting to recognize influences and desiring to know your innate desires is an incomparable option to choose. Glorious Meditates provides an option to dream, to visualize, to consider letting go of those perspectives that affect your emotions in unhealthy ways.

Meanwhile...

Human nature includes togetherness. These days, that might be a zoom call or something similar. It is the connection that matters; the sincere appreciation of connecting with someone, genuinely. You might think it odd that I refer to connection when Glorious is a solo lifer. That is because connection does not always have to be in person. Some people need space, they connect in their own way. Energetically, we are never alone, we are always connected. For me, sometimes feeling other people can be a bit much. However, I do recall family and other gatherings, and they were fun. Just as much fun is the space to be with my thoughts and be creative. Flowing with what life offers, excites me. This is why Glorious is a visual portrayal of what she experienced while meditating, she is flowing.

Life is about our experiences, and our opportunity to grow from those experiences. It is like childhood, which is our, organically, fresh eyes perspective part of life. It is when things are new, and learning is accepted as well as expected. At some point children know they are progressing to one day become adults, and adulthood can seem so enticing. I wish societally there was more emphasis on the beauty of childhood expressed to children as a norm. Emphasis on the opportunity to play, have more energy, and see life more purely can easily be lost in the message department of adult to youth lessons. Children get to have the whole rest of their (our) lives to be adults. Everyone gets to be a genuine child, once per lifetime.

Childhood-though not always appreciated while being experienced-goes by so quickly. Once it is gone, it never comes back. It takes us to the rhythm of adult life. A rhythm where we focus on our differences, a vibration where our commonalities can often slip by, barely noticed. Childhood to adulthood is a universal experience. It is beautiful to think about. The process can look so different to so many, yet, at the core, it is exactly the same.

Glorious Meditates fits into that category too. I wrote it wondering how many of us consider the fact that being that we live in a Universe, we are part of the Universe we live in. This fact, if embraced, leads to other recognitions. Such as, there are laws that exist in the Universe that are bigger than us. These laws are adhered to on some level, or we wouldn't exist. These are blueprint laws. Laws that are givens, that may often be taken for granted. Examples are the wonderful systems in place that sustain us. We live on a planet that constantly supplies us with air we can breathe, without question. This is true even though we (global society) seem to be testing that theory as if it's a game. There is gravity to keep us grounded. There is food to eat that grows best without our interference. There is so much to life that is for our wellbeing. Exploring possibilities can be an exciting pastime, or dare one consider: our life focus. I call these givens, part of my 21st Century P.E.A.C.E. Methodology; a blueprint for optimizing our life experience.

What does this have to do with Glorious Meditates? Everything, it is an example of my 21st Century P.E.A.C.E. (21P) techniques -Perspectives Embracing Agreement Cause Enlightenment. I am grateful the spiritual messages received during my youth awakened my awareness. Feedback and results carved my ability to explain the messages. In addition, (seemingly) random exposure to different theories began painting a picture that, when combined, provide the closest explanation of the Universal Laws I was awakened to. 21P is blueprint information, that applies to life. One might argue that it seems like 21P is nowhere. Like air. Think about it, if we didn't need air to breathe, would we usually notice it? 21P is simplicity. This is why Glorious Meditates can be enjoyed by many ages, generations, cultures, etc. It is a book for feeling good from the inside out.

The background imagery is my photograph with an oil paint vibe applied. This method was used to invite photography and animation to merge together more smoothly. Earth is an incredibly, beautiful visual being. I am grateful for Earth having patience with us. My intention is to share, uplift and mentally stimulate, while lighting curiosity to new heights.

Let your curiosity be set ablaze with a desire to experience more of life, like a surfer riding a wave desiring the wave to never subside. Like looking for your phone or keys that are already in your hand, Earth's beauty awaits your gaze. See delightfully, enjoy, be happy and share in the laughter of life as much as possible.

Peace,

Ra ✌️ 🟫 ?

Ready?

*You'll never find piece of mind
until you listen to your heart.*

George Michael

And here we go...

I can tell you're excited; again. What is it this time? You meditated and... oh, and speaking of meditation, you know what I am doing...

Yes, my calmly exciting favorite thing to do. You know this is my quiet time. You're one of my besties and you've been on my mind. I had to call and check on you.
Little did I know I would be delightfully responding to your need to share vibe.
I should have known. Good news is your thing.
I am in my backyard, relaxed. I am under the sun with my favorite beverage and you are on my speakerphone.
I am all ears...

with deciding which comfy clothes to wear. I wanted to meditate before it got too late...

It was dark by the time I was settled. As always, I began taking slow deep breaths in and out through my nose, directing the air down to my stomach. I held it there a moment each time before letting it out again. I did my best to think of nothing and to feel my breathing until I felt relaxation spreading through me from my core.

This signaled me that my mind was resting and I was consciously aligned with a higher Universal vibration, and aligned with Earth.

My love offering of respect was recognized and accepted. My inner travel was about to begin.

Inner expansion opened my innate guidance awareness as I consciously vibrated in love. From within, I began undeniably experiencing existence from a Universal perspective. I saw a city at night, with its glowing bright lights. It was quiet, the city felt like the peace I felt inside.

The thought running through me: "I am grateful".

Accepting my inner-peace, enhanced sensitivity to the love flowing endlessly through me. Not knowing it was a possiblity, I relaxed even more. Then I noticed it kind of felt like my love and my inner-peace were waiting patiently by the door. Obviously already acquainted, it was for my permisson they waited. Until now they'd been with me adoringly, knowing the opportunity to see was for me. Patiently, they waited. Time; undefined, was not a consideration. On my cue, they merged without hesitation. My fears, on vacation, were not around to alter the situation. So began the awakening of my peace and love comprehension.

It felt like my body said to me:
"Thank you", joyously.

The power of surrender driven awareness is peerless.
This knowingness flowed clearly through me, consciously,
as I felt focus formulating understanding in me fearlessly.
Articulation was soon to arrive. I was still processing what
I'd derived. Intentionally,
I was to let Peace be my
guide. Eventually, this
would cause ego and pride
to get so tired of trying
to drive my life ride.
Just as All Is Divine;
I am loved all the time.

Endless was the sky, I felt like I could fly, wherever, whenever I wanted. Joy flowed through me endlessly. Almost brought to tears, I realized I owned not an ounce of fear, and again it was clear, as the thought flowed through me, that, this...is...love.

Then click! A lock opened in my mind and it was clear that I knew all the time. Simplicity is the key. Our Universe is peace, that means, so are we. The distraction game is almost always the same, and we fall for it almost everytime.

Obvious distractions to keep us apart hurt humanity down to our hearts. One of our keys is recognizing lessons so we can see paths and master our progression. Negative or positive, all are for growth. The Universe watches patiently...This is woke.

I merged with nature as one texture and floated with my new knowledge. My meditation had peaked, I was feeling complete. My session would soon be ending.

The voice continued: "Trust and be logical like math. You're on your life path, needed keys will come your way. Breathe intentionally, listen to what your heart has to say. You will see your way. Others will benefit from what you say."

Perhaps for ease of transition, once again city lights at night were my vision. Appreciation of my relaxation, was paired with being grateful I retained the information. I was looking forward to a good night's sleep. I was relaxed, I was also beat. Responsibility to follow through ensured what I was to do. My heart was ready to share the knowledge everywhere with loving care.

I was ending my meditation with smooth, deep inhales, and belly exhales. I observed my brain burning to comprehend what I learned. My eyes, still at rest, had not opened yet. I had been energetically fed. It was time for me to go to bed.

I stood up, and stretched, happily, thinking this meditation was one of my best. Then I realized, with tired eyes, that I was really sleepy and needed to rest.

Warm and snuggled under my covers, I looked forward to going to sleep. And, oh boy! Did I! What happened next was deep.

Wow! We are incredible beings! More than we can dream. It's a truth no one needs to defend. We get to accept that we are more than we can comprehend. Let's open all our eyes, and recognize we are the prize. Collectively we create our reality. Our focus is top priority. Clearly, we are unlimited creativity.

I love it! Let's get this started! To support your consciousness mission, I will invite my empathetic folks with dough to experience one of your engaging awareness presentations. Let's go with your P.E.A.C.E. vibe: Perspectives Embracing Agreement Cause Enligtenment. It's time. I will get back with you to discuss your fees and expenses. It's funding time!

In case you have forgotten to dream, or how to dream, Glorious has your back. If a reminder that there are existing vibrations that surround you have slipped your mind, re-read Glorious until it is embedded in your psyche.

Hustle and bustle, electronic distractions, trends and opinions can seem like the important things in life, until ... you remember to remind yourself that you know that there is more. Even if you were never told, or never experienced that there is an incredible part of you that is not the norm to be discussed as an probability ... You know. Even if, your mind attempts to make it seem like it's your all and all; a part of you knows. It has to. It is part of you.

Similar to how you might not notice your nail, or your hair growing, or perhaps your body growing, it is, they all are. Whether you notice it or not, parts of you carry out their functions without prompting. Your brain, ego and emotions like to take create for those functions. Society supports that notion too, for the most part. That is, the popular part of society does. Sounding so believable, communicating with fingers crossed behind their backs like the way media portrays life as a constant succession of crime, murder and mayhem. Creating scenarios that one can attribute to lack of hope and despair. That is, until you think about it. Because, even in the most dangerous neighborhood, somewhere, somehow, there is light. There is hope. Even if that hope is based on knowing the sun will shine tomorrow. Even if you don't see it, you know the sun is in the sky. You know the sun is part of the Solar System we live in. That Solar System is part of a Galaxy, and that Galaxy is part of a Universe. All these systems are aspects of the thing we call life; following rules, and laws that are bigger than religion, politics, greed, economics, gender and race. What does this have to do with Glorious Meditates?

Meditation is giving yourself permission to let your mind rest and to consciously choose to be aware of your being. Truly taking this step is to recognize your youness without bias and own your aspects. It is an opportunity to see with real eyes that no matter if every single day were to come across as being exactly the same; it isn't, they aren't. If every single person on the planet has a unique fingerprint, and molecules are never still ... Those two aspects alone are evidence of opportunities that get to be recognized and embraced when one's mind is at rest. When meditation guides the way, revealing the wonderfulness of existence. Living can be seen and accepted as the irresitably unique experience that it is.

That is when choice starts screaming. Possibly, your brain and emotions will remind you of free will. Some call it one of the crossroads. It is easy to categorize this sort of mindset as woo woo, abstract thinking that has no purpose. Do you ever question, our life set up? Why is it that everything we need, absolutely need to live, is free? Is that not an example of a statement like; everything you need to live a healthy, stressless life is available to you for free.

The game is distraction from the benefits of inner fulfillment. What game do you choose to play?

It is second nature for many to use search engines to find word definitions. Hopefully, Glorious Meditates is engrossing you so much that you prefer to access all necessary information within the context of this book. Meaning reading paper pages is your preference right now. To assist with that desire, the following light glossary is available. It serves to define some of the abstract meanings that may be slightly different than the expected meanings.

Glossary

These definitions were obtained through many search engine sources. Most are stated as is, and are the second or third choice definitions. Also, some may be altered just a little to provide the definition that is intended for Glorious Meditates.

A

Accepted	Generally believed or recognized to be valid or correct. "He wasn't handsome in the accepted sense".
Acquainted	Someone aware of or familiar with someone or something. "New staff should be acquainted with fire exit routes". "Staff should be acquainted with their co-workers".
Adoringly	In a way that shows you love someone very much. "She gazed at her baby adoringly"
Aligned	Place or arrange in a straight line. Give support to (a person, organization, or cause).
Allness	Totality, completeness. The quality or state of being complete or universal.
Amazed	Surprised, astonished. "I was amazed that he could remember me".
Apologize	Express regret for something that one has done wrong. "I must apologize for disturbing you".

Appreciation	Recognition and enjoyment of the good qualities of someone or something. "I smiled in appreciation".
Articulation	Speaking in a clear, distinct, understandable way. Fully pronouncing each word.
Available	To do something.
Awakening	Becoming suddenly aware of something. Waking from sleep, (literally or figuratively).
Awareness	The state of being aware. Knowledge and understanding that something is happening or exists.
Awe	Of reverence, respect, and amazement.

B

Benefit	Something that promotes wellbeing.
Bliss	Complete happiness, joy.
Blooming	A person who is blooming has a healthy, energetic, and attractive appearance.
Boundlessly	Having no boundaries or limits. Vast.
Breeze	A gentle wind.
Burst	Impact or pressure within opening suddenly and forcefully.

C

Clearly	Easy and accurate understanding, perception, or interpretation.
Collectively	As a group, as a whole, as one. Teamwork.
Comprehend	To mentally grasp someone or something's (complete) nature; to understand.
Comprehend-ing	Mentally grasping someone or something's (complete) nature.
Comprehension	The act or action of grasping with the intellect: understanding.
Confused	Unable to think clearly; bewildered.
Consciously	Knowledge or awareness of one's own existence, sensations, thoughts, surroundings, etc.
Consideration	Kindness and thoughtful regard for others. Careful thought. Thoughtful and sympathetic regard.
Continued	Still happening, existing or done without a break or interruption.
Create	To bring something into existence. Cause something to happen as a result of one's actions.
Creativity	The ability to make or otherwise bring into existence something new.
Cue	Something done or said as a signal.

D

Deeply	Is highly pleasing, or a highly pleasing way or approach.
Defend	To protect. To take steps to prevent harm of another.
Delightfully	Is highly pleasing, or a highly pleasing way or approach..
Delved	To have searched, examined in detail.
Derived	To arrive at by reasoning and observation.

Distraction	Preventing someone from giving their (full or partial) attention to something or someone.
Divine	Excellent; delightful. Of, from or like God or a god.
Dominate	To have power, control or influence over someone, others, or something.

E

Ease	Absence of difficulty or effort. Being comfortable, able to live as you want, without worry.
Ego	One's conscious mind, the mental "I" or self that is the idea one has of their self.
Elements	Fundamental structure that cannot be easily broken into smaller pieces. Any of the 4 substances, air, water, fire, and earth, formerly believed to compose of the physical universe.
Embraced	To accept readily or gladly.
Endlessly	Having or seeming to have no end, limit, or conclusion.
Energetically	With a lot of energy.
Enhanced	To improve the quality, amount, or strength of something.
Enlightenment	Education or awareness that brings change, such as your enlightenment about nutrition that leads you to throw out your junk food.

Entanglement Theory	When 2 particles, ex: photons or electrons, become entangled, they stay connected regardless of distance or what's between them. They exist as one. A phenomenon in which entangled systems exhibit correlations that cannot be explained by classical physics. It has been suggested that a similar process occurs between people and explains anomalous phenomena such as healing. We can become entangled with anyone we encounter (Miller and Spiegel). This entanglement embeds itself in shared emotions, actions, and fears, suggesting that all human bodies (& existence) are interconnected to some extent.
Empathetic	The ability to sense other people's emotions, how they feel.
Eventually	An unspecified time when something will happen.
Excited	A state of energy, enthusiasm, eagerness … etc.
Exhaled	Sent air out of the lungs.
Existence	The state of being alive or being real.
Existing	Used to describe something that is now present, available or in operation.
Expanded	Increased size, number, or importance.
Experiencing	Something personally lived through or encountered.
Explicitly	A clear and detailed manner, without room for confusion or doubt.
Extraordinary	Very unusual or remarkable.

F

Fear	To be afraid of something negative happening.
Flowing	Moving smoothly and continuously in or as if in a stream or flowing water.
Formulating	To develop all the details of something, to express in precise form.

| Freedom | The quality or state of being free. |

G

Grateful	Deep appreciation of; kindness; being thankful. Gratitude.
Growth	Process of growing or developing.
Guidance	Advice, assistance, or counseling.

H

Healing	Achieving or acquiring wellness, the body's natural ability to repair itself.
Hesitation	Pausing before saying or doing something.
Hoard	To collect or accumulate things and closely guard them.
Humanity	The human race.

I

Incomprehensible	Not able to understand; not intelligible.
Incredible	Impossible or very difficult to believe.
Information	Knowledge gained from investigation, study, or instruction.
Innate	Existing naturally within rather than acquired. Existing before birth, thereby existing since birth.
Intensity	Extreme degree of strength, force, energy or feeling.

| Intentionally | Deliberately; on purpose. |

J

| Joyously | With undeniably happy feelings. |

K

| Knowingness | Strong, clever awareness and resourcefulness. No barrier exists between one, and what one knows. Knowing beyond conscious thinking. |
| Knowledge | Knowing something with familiarity gained through experience or association. |

L

Limitlessness	The quality of being infinite; without bounds or limits.
Lures	An attraction or appeal that pulls the person in a difficult to resist manner.
Luscious	Having a delicious taste or smell.

_M_

Meditation	An experience that takes you to the depths of who you are absent of thought.
Merged	To combine or cause to combine, to form as a single entity.

_N_

Natural	Not artificial or involving anything made or caused by another.
Nourishes	Providing what is needed for living healthy and for growth.

_O_

Observed	Noticed or perceived and registered.
Obvious	Easily perceived or understood, clear, self-evident, or apparent.
Oneness	The interconnectedness of everything.
Opportunity	Recognition of favorable circumstances.
Overjoyed	Extremely happy.
Overwhelmingly	In a way that is too powerful to resist.

P

Path	Course, route, a way of life.
Patiently	Tolerance for delays, problems, or suffering without becoming annoyed or anxious.
Peerless	Eminent beyond or above comparison. Unequaled; unrivaled.
Perhaps	Used when making a polite request, offer, or suggestion.
Permission	Allowing someone to do something.
Perspective	The way one sees, state of one's ideas; a way of thinking and understanding.
Pleasantries	Light, polite conversation or remarks.
Possibility	What may happen or be the case.
Pride	A feeling of deep pleasure or satisfaction from one's achievement(s) or another's achievement(s).
Priority	A thing that is more important than another.
Process	A series of actions or steps taken in order to achieve a particular end.
Progression	The process of developing or moving gradually towards a more advanced state.

R

Recognize	Identify someone or something from encountering, them (it) before.
Relaxation	Being free from tension and anxiety.
Respect	To feel or show honor or esteem for; hold in high regard.

Responsibility	Being accountable for or to take the blame for someone or something or a situation.
Retained	To hold or keep, recall, recognize; stored in memory information
Root	Basic source, cause, or origin.

S

Sensitivity	Easily offended; able to feel other people.
Signaled	An action movement or sound giving information to another.
Simplicity	The quality or condition of being easy to understand or do.
Simultaneously	Things happening at the same time.
Situation	A circumstance one finds their self in.
Snuggled	Settled in a warm comfortable position.
Stead	A substitute for another.
Suddenly	Quickly and unexpectedly.
Supported	Hold the weight of; give assistance to (including financially).
Surrender	To agree to stop fighting, hiding, resisting.

T

Texture	The feel, appearance, or consistency of a surface or substance.
Throughout	In every part of.
Transition	Changing from one subject, state, place etc. To another.
Trusting	Tending to believe in a person's honesty or sincerity.
Tuned	To be in harmony.

U

Undefined	Not clear or defined.
Undeniably	Emphasizes something cannot be disputed; a way that is certainly true. Plainly true.
Understanding	Comprehension.
Unhindered	Not obstructed; not held back or restrained.
Universal	Applies to all.
Unlimited	Not restricted.
Unparalleled	No equal, exceptional, no comparison.

V

Vibration	A person's emotional state; continuous quick, slight shaking movement.
Vibrantly	Full of energy.
Vision	Seeing scenes in your mind, an idea or mental image.
Void	An empty space; seemingly emptiness.

W

Within	Inside.
Woke	Aware of and actively attentive to cohesiveness, facts and issues.
Worthiness	The quality of being good enough.

Thank you
for being
Who you are
In the world!

Somewhere

in the Universe

where Earth

has been a hot topic

in many conversations;

a group of two

are discussing

their plan...

*She's quite impressive,
don't you think?*

*Well,
we have
been looking...*

*Yes indeed,
we have been
searching
for a while...*

*We will be reaching out
to her
when the time is right.*

www.ingramcontent.com/pod-product-compliance
Lightning Source LLC
Chambersburg PA
CBHW041700160426
43191CB00002B/39